GROUNDSPEED

AKRON SERIES IN POETRY

AKRON SERIES IN POETRY
Mary Biddinger, Editor

Titles published since 2008.
For a complete listing of titles published in the series,
go to www.uakron.edu/uapress/poetry.

GROUNDSPEED

Emilia Phillips

The University of Akron Press
Akron, Ohio

20   19   18   17   16   5   4   3   2   1

LIBRARY OF CONGRESS CATALOGING-IN-PUBLICATION DATA
Names: Phillips, Emilia, author.
Title: Groundspeed : poems / Emilia Phillips.
Description: First edition. | Akron, Ohio : University of Akron Press, 2016. | Series: Akron
   series in poetry
Identifiers: LCCN 2015048933 (print) | LCCN 2016002686 (ebook) | ISBN 9781629220345
   (hardcover : acid-free paper) | ISBN 9781629220352 (softcover : acid-free paper) | ISBN
   9781629220369 (ePDF) | ISBN 9781629220376 (ePUB)
Classification: LCC PS3616.H4553 A6 2016 (print) | LCC PS3616.H4553 (ebook) |
   DDC 811/.6—dc23
LC record available at http://lccn.loc.gov/2015048933

Cover: *Groundspeed* by Hollie Chastain, © 2015. Reproduced with permission. Cover design by
Amy Freels.

Groundspeed was designed and typeset in Centaur with Futura display by Amy Freels and
printed on sixty-pound natural and bound by Bookmasters of Ashland, Ohio.

Contents

"O brothers," I said, "through a hundred thousand
perils you have reached the West
and so, during this so brief a vigil
of our senses that remain for us,
be unwilling to deny the experience   .
of following the sun, the world unpeopled...."
—Dante's Odysseus

This car is just beginning its life. A lightning bolt couldn't stop it.
—Hazel Motes

for Janet, and for Tracy

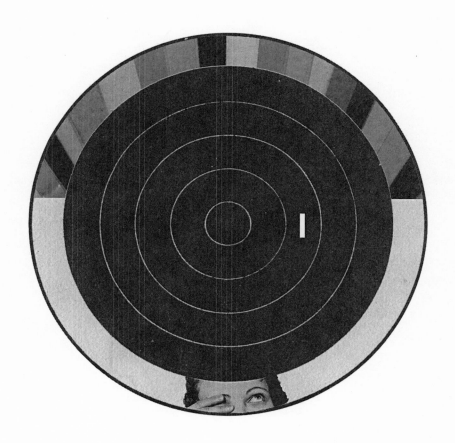

Reading Ovid at the Plastic Surgeon's

I scarcely dared to look
to see what it was I was.

No one else with a book, the slick
weeklies gossip amongst

themselves on the side
tables as the ticker rolls the Dow

Jones *down down down* under
a profile of the marathon

bombers (the older, a boxer). Jove
argues for the removal of a race

of peoples that do not please
him: *What is past*

remedy calls for the surgeon's
knife. He will take a hunk of my

cheek (cancer) and though I can't
see mid-procedure, I imagine

the site as an apricot, bitten.
This, a survival mechanism—

romanticism. David says,
If you're out

in public and you don't want anyone
to talk to you, bring a book

of poetry. Even as I enter the confidence
of the room, I avoid my

reflection in the window, for there,
most of all, I see myself as only I can,

as only the eye will have me—
as light, as light alone.

Life Vest Under Your Seat

At some indeterminate coordinate over the Atlantic,
the body sloughs hours like snakeskin, like one moral vestment

after another. An international flight is the closest
we'll ever know of limbo, from the Latin *limbus* meaning

hem or border. My email asks, *Did you mean to attach
files?* with the SEND-click of my response to my father's

photos: dust-colored mountains rostrumed on the walls
and metal buildings of Bagram. The in-flight entertainment system

has two flight cams: one from the nose, another from the tail.
The idea is, those of us who are comforted by knowledge

will feel safer seeing our vessel and where it's headed.
At night, only a regular tremor of wing lights. Nothing

else, but the dark variegated by clouds and lens dirt.
In Virginia where I live, our blond, zealot governor signed the bill

requiring an ultrasound before an abortion. My mother says
she's living only for *grandbabies*. But I'm living before then.

I am cold, and the blankets onboard are thin. A home
inventor in Massachusetts killed a young mother with his Shop-Vac

rigged for lipo. The hose snuffled up fat from her thighs
like cotton from a wet pillow. Is an accident always a purpose

of incorrect means? We need a control for these variables.
Let's say we know each other's pain and can sing along

with it like an old song. Let's say there's only one pain
performance but different seats in the auditorium.

On the set of *The Holy Grail*, Graham Chapman looked skyward
at a passing plane and said, *Think of all the gin and tonics*

they're having. This is how the other Pythons finally knew
he was a drunk. My mother got me sloshed

to teach me how to drink. Every time I fly now, I take half
a blue pill an hour before boarding. We have our hang ups,

our let downs, turbulence that rocks us to sleep. In case of a loss
in cabin pressure, overhead masks will drop, says the recording.

You've heard this before but not this: Claes Oldenburg used clippings
of legs from ladies' stocking ads for a study toward a giant

leather sculpture of shoestring potatoes falling from a sack.
Lately I've been thinking about how being an American means you're not

anyone else. This is how my friends know I'm an American. We declare
victory before we declare war. On a YouTube video, a singer signs a *V*

and licks between her fingers, the prosaic void. We know symbols
better than what they stand for. The evangelist my father was

named after touches a stranger's forehead out of time and says, *Heal*.
Limbus begot limb begot dismemberment. Blood splatter at the hand

of my father's colleagues in a Bagram lab becomes, simply, a scatter
plot. *Are you willing to help in the event of an evacuation?*

the man I used to call a steward says, tugging tight my seatbelt.
We are flying back in time, to the new world.

Stopping at Texaco a Year After My Brother's Death

In the fog the lot lights suspended
        I came out of a long

depression

into the middle of the night, here—

        entering a convenience

store with a gallon jar of eggs pickled
        canoptic

        in beet juice, brine, & vinegar

            beside an Atomic

        Fireball globe filled opaque

with caramels twisted in wax paper, the light

        tubular, *hospital*, an igneous
            clamor—

& left two pennies for the next

        customer & went on my way—

into the night, the highway,
this new life

like breath into the word mouthed into

the dead boy's ear.

Wheelchair in a Hayloft

see that there's nothing to see

I wouldn't have seen it had someone
        else in the car not pointed and said, *How*
    strange, and even then, it took me

a second to locate in the dilapidated barn's
        frame the passengerless chair wheel-
    locked in the hayloft at the sloping edge where

the front wall used to be, where it had
        fallen, so soft from the rain, into the creek
    below and dammed it so the grass at the corner

of the lot was swampy and ants floated
        or else drowned and the hornets beneath
    in their chambers drowned, their bodies

sometimes rising through the soil to the
        surface so you could go to them and pick
    them up and hold them between your

fingers and press the stinger into your arm
        without breaking the skin, their wings
    like corn husk but more rare and faceted

like an eye and I knew all of this the moment
        I understood what it was I was looking for
    and what I was looking at and although I saw

the chair up there for just a moment as we
             passed I did not see it for what it was, I saw myself
      wheeling out my brother's, riding the elevator

to the garage, the balloon tied to the arms,
             its smiling face like that of a polite stranger who
      asks, without judgment, if I'm headed up or down.

Pastoral (Future Interstate)

Under a tattered billboard, horses

graze. A shadow   the shape of a cloud

schooners the grass. The screws   in my heel

tighten. It will rain in several

miles. A call,   a message: a voice

separating from   time like ice

broken, washed   downstream.

Entente

Watching my mother tweeze a tick from her vulva,
        its body like a tumid berry drupelet vised within
the dermal pleats, inflaming them florid—
        I first knew I was other, and in my otherness, felt more

        for myself than I'd yet. I was ten. Separate yet tender.
Mind, nerve. On the closed commode, she eyed
        the nudnik swimming in place against her and beaked
at it, spreading herself, the muumuu gathered at her bosom.

I refused to move from the cold edge of the tub,
        soaking cotton in rubbing alcohol as she instructed,
though I was frightened—by her

woolly gulf and what wouldn't let go, love born
        swift to toothe into my softness, the sympathetic verve
that first beget the endless plump & suck of *I know.*

Abstinence Lesson

Mrs. M. thumbed Scotch Tape on the backs of our hands: mine,

quint-crowned in Zanzibar blue, chipped and chewed, fidgeting
through Girls' Studies, "The Sex Unit." *A woman is like a piece of*

tape, she began. *When she touches her first, she sticks;*
when she's removed, she is less

capable of sticking again. We ripped in unison—
but the remainder lace of hair and skin was too much

of us, or too little, a sign of something we weren't just yet
and something we had always been: hint and redaction.

By then, I was infatuated with a man twice
my age and had begun to hold my body like a pitcher of ice

water on a mirrored tray. But even this isn't the whole
story. No story is. But so goes its sad and open end:

Nights, I parted myself with the hairbrush's smooth handle,
turning to the wall, cold on my cheek, beside my twin

bed and rocked against the guilt lioned by the need.

The Showers

White noise of water and foot

slaps across the floor flooded

by sixteen showerheads the women

bathe under, undressed as strangers,

their rented towels hung with prismatic

swimsuits like nation-flags, along

the wall. I stuff my locker

with Levi's, my sweater, the bra

and panties he likes best

but I don't go in the aqua-

tiled showers naked but chilled

in a two-piece, the open

spray breaking against my body

draining through the floor.

2.

There's no delicate way to say

this—he asked to have another

join us, and so we've spent

hours weighing the hypotheticals—

the café girl who tonged

the *skinka og osti* croissant steaming

from the industrial oven, a friend

of mine, *his*, a stranger

from a bar. None of

these. The sign reads: *Your body*

is covered in salts and oils. In

the spray, I can barely

see anyone. I will pass

unwrecked. No one sings.

3.

Keine mehr Seife! says the woman next

to me as she combs her

pubic hair with long oyster-

colored fingernails. *Haben sie . . . ?*

and, looking at me—*Soap?* My

mother walked through

the house in the mornings nude

searching through unfolded

clothes, eyelids already charcoaled,

lips greased ruby. At twelve, I mimed

gagging, hiding under the bed to

watch her at the clouded vanity

mirror, zaftig and familiar, mist

herself with White Diamonds.

4.

There's nothing beyond her twin

bed cushioned in the down

of memory, her hair-scent and sleep-

breathing, the world turned out with

the light. There's nothing to tell. The morph-

ology of desire's dead end. *Nothing*

happened, though I wanted her. My body

was heat radiating. We were clothed,

the two of us, in the dark. I woke

before her and locked myself

in the bathroom to shower

and dress. (He wasn't there.) In the mirror,

I saw myself break open like water,

I saw but didn't feel the shiver.

The Bright Obvious

After Fukushima, my
       father in Kandahar
had shipped to
       me a box of paper

masks and a bottle
       of res-
       veratrol,
a compound
       found in Japanese
knotweed and grape skins
       that mends

       wrecked
cells, from the glottis to funny

       bone scales. My dog has
a tumor inside her
       nose that was supposed

       to kill her
two years ago but has only made her
       snore. In *Dorian,*

Wilde wrote: *What is Art?*

       —*A malady.* Last night,

my neighbor's father,
       a missionary
to Uganda, puffed a cigar

on the deck that connects
                    to ours. We all have
            cancer, he told me. It's just
            a matter

of where. I expected him to
            say the same's true

for faith. But he only looked out
            at the yard,
            at the grass that won't
grow but stays seed and mud,
            and puffed.

                        Each time I go to
the doctor, she examines the mole
on my cheek and I feel a tingle
            as if something's
on the move—
                    the brown lump

        changing
because she looked and still
            she looks,
taking my chin into her cold hands.

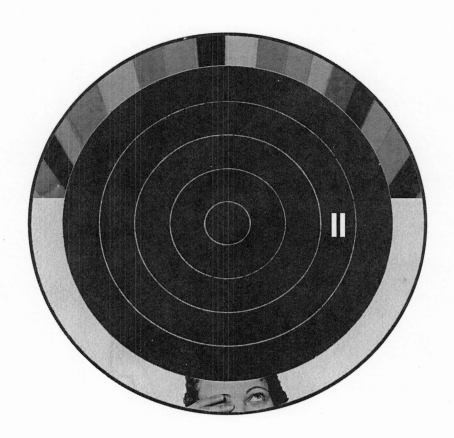

YouTube: Dog Eating a Human Leg on the Ganges

—a prayer

And who would
       stop it? Water heals
around the rock
       on which it tears
       fat slack-lining
              muscle, skin, & dries
       in the sun burning a
              white eye into
       the camera
              phone held by a man
       who begins
              talking to others
or to me, and the dog
              turns, hearing
       the voice, and I
              know then if
you approached
              it would not be
afraid or change
              even for the moment
you wrap your
              arms around
its neck & burrow
              your nose into
the sweet-sick
              fur, kiss, and unto it
breathe a soul
       of your
own conception.

Lodge

When the Sleepwalkers at dawn finally stumble into their rooms or slump over the steering wheels of their hubcapless Impalas, the seagulls land and become a landscape over a landscape, as snow does: a contour line, a living topography of the Budget Inn on the corner of N. Lombardy and Brook in Richmond. When the flock lifts, it lifts at once, proportional to its placement across the steep roof, the cars, and the open lot, so it seems something essential, even soul-like, rises— the way in movies a ghost flickers over a body at death: superimposed blue, see- through and shining: confused, maybe even smiling, until it looks around and sees itself, or who it was, there, on the ground.

*

I dreamed I wandered lost in a city in only a lace nightgown, a blanket over my shoulders. I'd escaped a high-rise hotel after an elevator crashed into the basement, a column of fire rising and lashing through the steel doors on the top floor, the stairs blocked by avalanche. I don't remember how I got out, and therefore wasn't sure I had. (Was I a ghost? a projection?) I came to on a sidewalk in a deserted part of town (the buildings boarded up, the garbage in heaps on the curb uncol- lected) without knowing where I was or where I was going. But then I found my car double-parked, running, the key in the ignition.

*

Today, two suns: one in the rearview, one in the side mirror. The meter money rattles in the door to the bass drum on Feist's "The Bad in Each Other." As I turn a corner, my shadow laps me.

Frank Zappa wanted to buy up billboards along the Eisenhower Interstate System and plaster them with two words: DOUBT EVERYTHING.

✲

✲

I drive from Richmond to Raleigh, Raleigh to Fredericksburg to Gettysburg on two-lane highways for two days. I keep my notebook open on my lap to write down the names of motels I pass, partly because they've devolved from Technicolor postcard destinations with mod geometric signs to roadside slumps of peeling paint and mediocre marquee promises.

ROYAL INN
Waterbeds

CRESCENT MOTEL
*Clean Room * HBO*

360   M
        O
        T
        E
        L

CARDINAL MOTOR COURT
Travelers Welcome
Micro Fridge

JOHNSON'S LODGE
Vacancy / Single Double / Color TV

My late anxieties become totem: unrest, excess, (anonymity).

＊

Driving from Gettysburg to the Baltimore Amtrak, I listened to a Hopkins radio segment on the link between sleep cycles and depression. A neurologist advised listeners that emotional health could be improved by turning off the television and computer at least two hours before bed, as electronic screens emit a blue light whose rapid frequency fools the body's circadian into thinking it's a time for wakefulness, a bright re-beginning.

＊

One summer, at age ten or eleven, I couldn't sleep and so watched the full run of Nick-at-Nite, *Lucy* at nine to *Mr. Wizard* at five, sucking on Mayfield banana popsicles and chipping away at Rita's Italian ices with a tongue depressor, crawling beneath the uncurtained back windows from the den to the kitchen so no one, no intruder surely there, could see me. My mother, clinically depressed, slept all night with a hair dryer on to drown out noise; she held it like a drowsy cowboy on watch with his gun. I was terrified, and rightly so, of fire. And so I stayed awake, for when I closed my eyes I saw her shadow moving down the hall, eyes aflame, smoke sibyling from her mouth.

＊

The insomniac speaker of Larkin's "Aubade"—terrorized by this thought:

> *The sure extinction that we travel to*
> *And shall be lost in always. Not to be here,*
> *Not to be anywhere,*
> *And soon; nothing more terrible, nothing more true.*

For three years I've had bouts of nighttime terror: about my ten-year-old half-brother's death and my diagnosis of stage-four melanoma a year later. With cancer, it helps knowing where the cells are; when one doesn't know, *Not to be here,* one feels one can't control it, contain it.

With my brother's death, my great transgression—which I grieve but cannot help—has been to imagine his body underneath the soil, in his last Halloween costume, a Superman uniform, the pre-mortem atrophy turned post-mortem decomposition. I wish he were ash. *Not to be here, / Not to be anywhere,* so that he could be free again to dwell in thought.

*

When dark times loom, we cliché. *Night is coming.* Whenever we have hope, we cliché. *I see the light at the end of the tunnel.* Both used as metaphors for the approach of death.

*

Once, a black bag wheeled out of the Budget Inn. Police tape cracked like a whip in the wind. Another time, another day at the red light, I looked through an open door, second from the end; inside, a shirtless man with Mansonesque beard and hair danced in front of the television rabbit-eared to the news.

*

GET YOUR DAILY EXERCISE
RUN AWAY FROM SATAN

GRAVEYARDS ARE FULL
OF GOOD INTENTIONS

EXAMPLE IS A LANGUAGE
ANYONE CAN READ

(recent favorite church marquees)

*

My mother's story:

The father of my first best friend, the preacher at the Grace Reformed Baptist Church, asked me, age four, if I'd died that day, where would I go, *Heaven or hell?*

I answer again and again in the retelling: *My mom doesn't let me go places like that by myself.*

*

Roadside signs, line breaks original.

28

MAGIC TOUCH
All
Girl Staff

FLYING CIRCUS
AIRPORT

AMERICAN EX-PRISONERS
OF WAR HIGHWAY

*

On the lobby RCA, a football game in whiteout conditions in the snowy reception of antennas where we lose the players in a huddle.

On an unsalted stretch, bested by ice, I submit to $51.00 /night and color television at the Boston Inn in Westminster, Maryland, the only place open. The incandescent light reviving a moth's orbit that had stilled in the darkness preceding my artless entrance on the chain gang of shadows, anxious and shaking. My pack slumped on the chair. The odor fecal, of cigarettes. My mind wanders: *Whose knees were burned on the geometric carpet?* A hole melted into the bedspread's vanitas of flowers. The deadbolt latches but the doorframe's busted, gold chain thin as a necklace. My tire tread caked in snow.

Entering this room, I enter a room inside myself with four corners and a human form, crouched in a shadow, the bathroom light falling on me and falling on me again in the mirror. I want to hear the form speak to me, my own voice echoing off the tile before I leave with a refund, but as I recall absence can only be heard by dogs.

*

Abandoned churches. A one-room wooden with peeling white and copper-green paint, broken glass windows, on Mt. Olive Lane in Southern Virginia. Alongside the *No Trespassing* signs, a little one:

FUTURE HOME OF
The Wedding Chapel

The other's outside Biglerville, Pennsylvania. I barely got a look at it, except its yellowed marquee:

NEW
HOPE
CHURCH

*

Bachelard: "It is better to live in a state of impermanence than in one of finality."

Which is why it is better to live in language rather than out of language.

But a word might change us, our landscapes, our movements. As if by traveling on the interstate, we might actually move between states of being.

*

On our way to see our first place in Richmond, we got lost on a street that was the same name as the street we were supposed to be on but the two didn't connect. As we were driving, slowly to see the numbers, I caught sight of a woman on the concrete porch of one of the craftsmen. She had on several layers of skirts in autumn colors, a peasant shirt, her hair wrapped in shimmery purple. She looked like one of the vintage coin-op fortune tellers, a *gypsy*, although I have never seen a real gypsy, and worry now even calling her that I'm buying into America's greatest product: kitsch.

She beckoned to us, waving come in, come in, come in.

✻

I fantasize about inventing a downloadable voice setting for GPS: VIRGIL™ who might provide us with more insightful directions. *Ex. You will leave everywhere I guide you, we hope.*

✻

A partial concrete list of my abstract fears:

Vibrating bed. Shag carpet. Black-light forensics. Synthetic waffle batter hissing on a press at the continental breakfast. Candy bars in the mini-fridge with the little bitty bottles of Jack. Bedbugs. Plastic mattress covers. Oily telephone receivers. Bedside table Bibles. Peed-in pools. Sticky and/or stained sheets. Fist-sized holes in the wall. Bullet-sized. Busted-in door frames. Snapped door chains. Snuff films. A friend's coke cut on my bedside table. Thin walls. Thin doors. Peepholes. Hair in the drain. Unidentified fluids. Unknowns, ineffables. *Unspeakables.*

✻

The preacher, I remember, had a waterbed.

I wonder, was it to be more like Noah?

I've always sympathized more with the unnamed thousands, millions who died in the flood, who didn't believe Noah or in the coming apocalypse. I like to think they weren't jaded with God but rather hopeful that they would keep what they had, that they wouldn't get washed away. Their bodies are never mentioned, not during the flood. Not after the ark lands. I like to think that those people lived, in a kind of Calvino-esque city, a world under the surface world—permanent against the changeable winds, the temporary currents.

✻

So many of the old tourist motels outside of Gettysburg National Park are now low-income apartments. Often, driving home in the early evening, I'd spot residents in the parking lot igniting charcoal in a scrap-metal grill with lighter fluid.

A baby draped over a shoulder like a rifle.

A car hood up.

Or no one at all.

One still has a vending machine, the only light for a mile.

✻

I pass an empty field bordered by trees, a tattered billboard in its center:

Future Home of the
FOUNTAIN OF LIFE

*

Before my mother married him, my stepfather—addicted to pain pills, recovering with pain pills after a car wreck caused by falling asleep at the wheel after a handful of pain pills—lived in the Extended Stay America. We would bring over beef tips and baked potatoes from Steak-Out and eat them out of to-go Styrofoam, *Law and Order* on the television.

Before that, we lived with my father near a cemetery, the thought of which, lingering just beyond the dark shape of the woods, would keep me up at night, as if ghosts could travel underground and rise into my room like radon. I had recurring nightmares of tombstones erupting through the floorboards.

A cemetery seemed then as much a transient space as a motel, or a mobile home like where my husband grew up.

These places seemed not to create life, but carry it.

Static, Frequency

A lash across the bandwidth bedstead—

my radio superego led by *heel, toe, dosey*

doe. Memories aren't

mercy, even if they rescue

you into innocence. I wish it wasn't easy

for the body to think I've suffered

because I sweat in front of a gym TV

on which St. Louis police

draw on another young man. Because I wince,

because I'm grateful

there's no sound, because empathy

is always a bad overdub, don't

trust me. I'm running

from no one. On the closed

captioning: [*man shouting*] OH

MY GODD! This is America,

where few witness

and most watch. I keep

running toward it

without ever getting there.

[*static*] Nights

I listened to that station in my twin

bed, country had nothing

to do with land but with

boundaries. Silence was

an inheritance I didn't know

I'd received. Did I sing

for my father & his cop

buddies *bullets* & *My-babies*?

Officers, I'm getting

nowhere. Officers, I have to

know: would you have fired?

Would my father? I sang

at the dinner table: *get down, turn*

around. I knew the words then

but didn't (didn't I?)

know the song.

Pastoral (Oncoming)

The tired eyes dilate to let in more

    light. The broken line flames

        white columns that hit the vanishing

            point with the regularity of a metro-

                nome as I swerve, uncertain of the curve,

                    and headlights ahead and behind against

                        the mirrors explode asphodelic.

The Episode of Cops *in Which*
My Father Appears

never aired. The suspect surrendered
               his life. No suicides on basic
cable, no mortal wounds or use. Only pump-
               action and hacked kilos,
         the call girl's doughy blurs,

and the swing pixeled between a pantsless perp's
               scramble—its reel
         quickened at the end
credits to match footfall
         with the rhythm of *Bad boys / bad*

         boys. Not my father

on the radio after the shot's flash-coil
in the House of Windows or the bullhorn
               answered
by silence, the hostage (the suspect's
               fiancée) and her scream too

         like a hostage
let loose as she returns
         from the bathroom—
to find him a spray, mouth open, funny

         she'd never
seen his teeth, not all of them, not that he
               had
all of them, capped in some cheap

metal, his rat tail precious as a lock
        in a Bible.
Or the women outside the chicken

processing plant: no, we won't see them
waiting around for the blinking and winking meal bells
        (AM/PM) for the boys that like to
make jokes about breasts and thighs.

Some women
        lose what little they have
in the backseat after a sting.
        Wash your hands.

        Wash your hands of this.

        My father leaning against
the counter in my grandmother's kitchen with a Yogi
        Bear jelly jar of milk the color
            of his undershirt, almost
as translucent, after listening to my bad
        day at school, drained

the glass and said, *At least*
        it wasn't a body stewing
in a house for a week, at least it wasn't my tangent on that—
        the body's cat
nibbling at its earlobe like a lover, like someone
        who would do whatever
you wanted them to do on the bench
        seat of the pickup, at gunpoint, in the rain

        or no rain

there was to dapple and fog
  the lens, if only you had the right words
instead of these negotiations
to open the door instead
  of kick it in.

The Wind Lends a Voice to the Mountain Laurel Above Pretty Polly's Grave

...And shook the shady honours of her head
—Ovid's *Metamorphoses*, Book I

Scarce I'd said my last prayer when through

my body spread a dragging blackness like a root

through a skull— Since then I've had nary

a word for the hills and valleys or the river where my daddy's

mill wheel turns the black water to power

but an ear's a deeper ravine than that between Here-and-There

and it carries an echo So I'll tell you I saw Willie again yesterday

He came in a suit, hair oiled To his chest

he pinned a bloom to impress I know not who

All These Things Shall Be Added Unto You

St. Pete's

In chapel I castled in air a flood
from rain that forked on the windows

silver and sheeted in gusts
to mirrors flashing moments,

and although the school was
citadeled on a hill, I imagined the halls

as canals I paddled with canoes carved
from pews—my oars

the crucifix and torch, my life
vest fashioned from the Common

Prayers. I camped in
the rafters and made hand-sized fires

of palms ignited by match and oil. At night I
would drink myself to my first

drunk on communion
red and spread Peter

Pan on the wafers. My daydream then
was not of love, though the stairs

became a waterfall, the computer monitors—
conchs on the lakebed, silent,

their green hypnotic
now dark. The organ pipes were dead

coral that burbled when I dove
from the nave to plunge

its keys. I once said
that prayer was the first form

of love
poem I knew, but before prayer there was

absence. I drowned the other
sticky children

pewed alphabetically
on either side of me

in absence—their bodies not
floating face down, unrescued by their parents

or the Coast
Guard. They were simply

gone with the flash flood
like the masses in Noah's time that we never heard

knocking against the hull
or discovered in trees

bloated and winking, petal-eyed
like Benny Goodman.

Noah didn't survive
long after the ark. The water,

we know now, was
poisoned by us.

Strata

After a dig archaeologists toss something of this
    world in the backfill so later excavations aren't
        nuanced by earlier efforts: a water bottle, Lay's
            bag; at Hisarlık, a joke, a Trojan in its chintzy foil.

The object not *of*, but *now* & ordinary, indelible.
    All the great finds then must be marked
        by the out-of-context. A walking stick dropped
            in terror or awe by a laborer at Lintong, or—

tune in to the image of Howard Carter's revolver
    in its final resting place a km outside Tutankhamen's. Soon
        the new archaeologists will dig for the old archaeologists,
            their Timexes, travel Scrabble tiles & ink wells, & unopened

cans of beer or beans, popped footballs & pocket
    change that mark the long catalogue of half-advances,
        half-defeats in looking for gods or man, whichever
            came first or last—or them between.

Tomography

Mundane most
        pain but worsened
for worry. In the blurry
        tube arcs
the ray

        in its literal, invisible

halo. Always a
        hallowing, *to know*—Early

missionaries couldn't halve
        abstraction from the concrete
for the Chinese

        as each discarnate
dwelled
        in *hanzai*, materialized

in symbol—
        here

my body's
        remade, pixel
by gray scale
        pixel, and still,
nothing more

        defined

for me inside
        of me, though the oncologist
circles the sentinel

        node
and offers his fists
        to illustrate   *(here's the
church, here's the*

        steeple)
how the body fates itself

        by how

and what

        it divides.   *(look at all the people)*

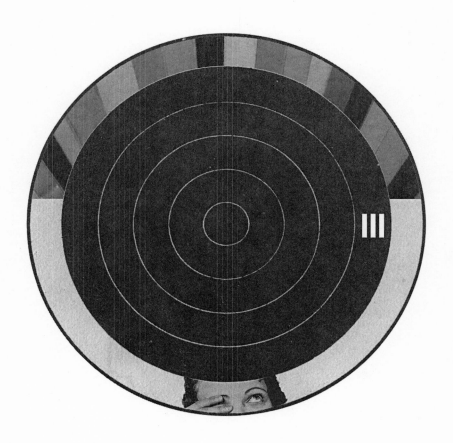

"The Rising Cost of Dying"

—headline

The man without half his
          jaw holds
his tongue,
          molaring it into his one
true cheek as if it would lash
          out, venomous,

if let go of

          like an arrowhead
snake released
          from finger and thumb—

The crowded basement
                    waiting

room with its undercurrent
          of less-a-lung
breathing and machine-
          hum, the benign

quinine smell of gauze
          cocktailed with failing

bodies' sharp furtive—
          crushed

juniper, soured white
          pepper. His rough
hands that rub

                              the slack
            jowl, deboned, without
                    stop—

        as if it still surprises

                    —and it *does*—

            though he looks
from surgery a while
            healed, or healed
enough, the flesh almost not
            his without

structure like a dress or shirt
                        once tailored to fit now
            with all the hems let out.

                              . . . I must look
            like the healthiest one here and worry
                        their whispers about me—

                        Young and

        plump,
                    what's she

                    need?
            But in my groin, a clutch
                of pains, berrylike

            in their spheres, each hard as a nut—
another under my arm, the scar

on my cheek waxy,
healed, though it sears

in the night against the pillow.

They'll take so much
    this time
        they'll have to
            rebuild, jigsaw
from behind my ear, my neck—

    A doctor
once had my grandmother scissor
    swatches from each
of my mother's shoes and affix them to her
    back for a week without shower
    to see if she would break out,
        allergic—

But it was the glue
        on the masking
tape that caused the rash, her shoes—
    tongueless.

The man
    in the reflection
on the receptionist's scratched
    window

    rubs and rubs
the doughy cheek, callus

    against whisker
    as another

man in profile
        looks
whole in the television
        changed

from the news to the weather.

Pastoral (With One's Head out the Car Window)

Although drizzle nettles the cheeks red

& one's ears fill with wind's grey-green noise—

there's clover & honeysuckle, the cheeks held

intimately by almost nothing. Once, everything

we couldn't understand was made through similes

of nature. Now the trees look like telephone

poles. A wingspan, a hanging up receiver.

Phaeacia's Orchard

—a version

Behind the Craftsman, a hundred feet from the screen
    door, the orchard stretched an acre deep, chicken wire
strung along its length, post to post, between our

    yards. The trees tangled & diseased, though enough remained
to waste & what fell with juice contusioned, softening
    where it rested until the sun, if it made it

through, roiled their upsides to split and spew, fermented seep—
    a taste in the wind that, before a storm, combed the leaves
to their pale undersides like the blighted backs

of knees revealed by a windblown skirt. Red & black
    plums, Alleghenys crowding apricot as the poor peaches beggered
the sun. Inside the Kings' fireplace two tires waited for

    winter beneath a black rose of soot on the mantel. And here
in the side yard, a flower garden fit for a court, & beyond it, the tilled
    rows of beans. In curlers his wife trampled the sunflowers

after flushing her lithium. The plums first reddened
    like the cheeks of Eros & then darkened as if to bruise,
& there by the last rows, a compost heap held the fallen

    fruits from which the flesh shrugged off the pit, glistening,
& sticky, & host to fly & beetle & nit year
    in, year out. And last, there was a ditch rippling in spring

with rain flooded fluorescent by pollen, that dried in summer
    & revealed a half-buried empty can of candied yams & the fossils
of his boot from when he stumbled in & drew

water into his sock. Such was the affluence of our neighbor's
orchard, the glories of their mundane. And there I stood
    at the fence, handed one after another plum by Mr. King,

my arms deltaed in sweet, until we were both called
    back inside by screams that'd borne so much, in their gaze.

Bruce Bickford at the Edge of the World

American stop-motion animator, 1947—

As a kid I would look into the valley

below our house and hope all the little

buildings and the trees, the mailboxes, sheds

and the eensy people were as tiny

as they seemed. The soul has no

concept of the size of the body, except through

motion. But in motion, we are larger than when we are

still. Sometimes I'd think, I'm going

down there to see how big things

really are. But I was afraid everything would be

regular sized. Countries shouldn't go to war

with one another. They should make movies about going

to war with one another. The soul is the

momentum of the body, the body the residual motion

of the soul. If you're at the edge

of the world, I bet you can

put your hands right

into the earth and begin to

mold it stretch it until it's not

an edge at all anymore.

Snake Woman

A buck for an adult, 50 cents a kid

      to ascend the aluminum steps

of the wagon half Winnebago, half

      horse trailer parked on the edge

of the Va. state fair fringed in pasture

      funk, the dead mines of dung

cake co-morbid with pickup truck

      exhaust, smoking peanut oil. The lion's

share pro-Romney–Ryan with their double-

      frittered Twinkies and red

velvet-battered rattler, *Fresh from*

      Texas. She has the head of a beautiful

girl & a serpent's body, is painted

      to look like Bettie Page on the vehicle's

tinny shell, and yet she's a shaved

        head and concrete tail affixed in a boa's

circle. She sits on a wooden stool

        beneath the stage, half-woman, half-

ophidian. An altar to our grotesqueries: chewing

        gum and a gaze fixed on the sky full

of smoke and storm. At last she blows

        a bubble for us, with us—

it pops. An Angus bull across the aisle, blue

        ribboned for its weight.

Groundspeed

A falling plane as vessel. As Valkyrie—

The espresso shots tremble, darkening; the ounces
chatter on the tray as the unceilinged twin-
engine roar scourges the ear of the drive-thru
worker who only made out *double tall*. Out the window,
    the plane jerks kite-like, tether whipped serpentine, &
drops like an elevator into the abandoned strip mall's
      parking lot a block from the register, nose snapped like
pencil lead guided by the god-hand that wanted to write
          something (elegy, condemnation) across the weedy
& scarred blacktop. The falling plane is thrall, apologia of who's
    to become shadow. After hours, she guided us outside
with chilled canisters of heavy cream sweetened with vanilla
          pressurized to spray. It was her last
night on the job. I used to dream I could float two stories
    high, confetti above a fire barrel, but when I
addressed my grounded companions, they said, *You're not*
        flying. When I say, *tangible*, I mean, *to*
touch. I mean, *Of the earth* & not above it. & yet love

    is an act of falling; & parting, falling out. The sirens like planets
revolving their distant tracks. I saw into the distance
through sound, not sight. Would you believe
    the plane carried survivors?

Whatever crashes downwards, sends praise back up . . .

A transference of energy—   Having buried
    itself as far into the ground as
proportional to its strength per the ground's density, the force reverses &

tremors back through its messenger. One night in front
of the glass storefront, a man shoots another. The blood horizons the body,
    like light
on the edge of the world. The bullet wanting more, wanting to pull all the way
through the abdomen, like stone through water, as it stretches the tissue a final
    half
millimeter before coming to rest.
                  It was September & the wind was
hot through the window. Our hands were soft with milk, sour.

We watched the wreckage catch
        after the pilot & passenger crawled
out. The plane as elegy.   A body
can, like a sympathetic string, ring with another's
            peril. The falling plane like a horn player's
air, following the arc of the instrument, narrowed, condensed into
    movement, to pure recognizable, and then, mid-sustain,
    the mouthpiece yanked away from the lips—the sound
bottoms, and what was note is now only breath that scatters....

    Reach now from the edge of Lookout
Mountain to a ledge below, for the glasses the girl dropped...
    Survive the body.

So many histories have their falling Gods. So many Sires put their sons in
chariots—
    with a bridle of free will, a bit of pride slobbered over.

Every time I write *son*, I want to write *song*. When I write *fall*, *fault*.

The system's bass beat in the side mirrors. The reflection in the car's roof—

For the moment, nothing but the overhang of the café's drive-thru & the sky,
an arc of what one, at a glance, leaning out, one would name as a bird, buried
colorless.

The falling plane as a reversal. As revival. Jamichael and I huddled at the
        propped-open window,
after our customers were gone & the road was closed & emergency workers
swarmed like stars. The only arrivals were a hot wind that scaled the flames
        like a mountain & the scent of aftermath, the little gods in the raindrops,
        & our bodies expanding through pain we had not felt. The smoke
was like a great chain

that held the sky to the earth. It was just far enough in the distance to be in
the distance, for us to feel we were there before we realized we weren't.

Paradiso

On the edge of our window
        table, light through
glass refracts. Two
        bottles. We break

bread and fill
        our saucers shallow, eat
until on the street

        below, a car
hammerheads into
        a bicycle, the rider's
leg rag-wrung
        in aluminum
frame undertread.

        Squeal—
the brakes, and down
        the hood the body
        skids....Crack
and recoil. Pavement.

        Driver and his
passenger unbuckle. The mussels
        steam open. To your lips,
you touch your
        napkin, turn

away. Inverted, the scene in
        the bottles
gleaming. Vinegar,
        oil.

Saul Bass Redesigns the First Man

I want to make beautiful things even if nobody cares.

To make, you first have
        to create materials. Re: MAN, we know
the rib removed. But, *before*——?
        Forget *ash to ash, dust*
        &c.

                Stick a floating rib (i.e., thoracic
11–12, y'know—"Edenic") in a glass
        of water with the promise
                it'll grow
        roots like leek or fur

                like chia. The joke's Crusoe
        astride the bone or Jim & Huck paddling
rustic as a ballpoint pen will go.
        —*Nn-o.*
                (*That's not a plank*
                        in your peeper!) —

        It's a hollow; *cue*: running

faucet, a Pabst-crack opening
                into seraphic
        choir. (Risk Handel's?
A perfect major? root, third, & fifth?) With aesthetics,
        like a bad comb-

                over, you don't
        need a mirror to know what you are
missing. Now that you have this
        thing, you've got to

feed, roof, & rock-

a-bye baby. You're the big boss, head hauncho

O, but watch out, foreman, Little Evie
& Adam were the first
organized union. (*1-2-3-4...*

don't give us pain in labor!)

So what'll you give him in return?

Latin and genus?
Genius?
...Medicinal plants?

(*I call this "Vladimir*
Nabo-cough," man.)

Or do we let him take for him-
self by fount,
fin, & medium—language. Though from this,
we know
creation is only

myth; destruction, narrative.

Roadside America

Where was I going with no other map than a mirror?
—Pierre Martory

Every year Jesus looks more
like Jesus, as a word

sets into the shape
of the word and less the shapes of

its letters once one understands
what it means. In Texas

a bowling alley was converted
into a church with twelve

altars and waxed floors that held
the icons of the saints

looking at their shoes. In the lot, a hand-
painted billboard: *JESUS* in red

futuristic script. But the future
the artist on his ladder and harness

proclaimed in the uvular curve
of the *U* never came. The future now

dated, like every end
of the world. Apocalypse is a matter

of scale. The model
town of Roadside America in Shartlesville, Pa.,

met its first doomsday when the leaky roof
caved into the Wild

West, crushing the mill, eroding
the range, and scattering the cattle.

At half-past the hour, the lights dim for "God
Bless America" as an Anglo-

Nazarene is projected over Lady Liberty
painted on the far wall. Her robe

giving His texture, her torch become the Bible.

I believe absurdity is a miracle.
In the pale undersides

of leaves before a storm, I glance the shape
of *Boiled Peanuts* and *Ajax*,

the parable of the paper doll
thumb-tacked to a corkboard.

On every windy hill
along I-75, an aluminum cross blinds

drivers with sunlight. This is evangelism—
as are pies, blue lights, and return

address labels. One day Jesus will
look so much like Jesus we won't

be able to recognize him.
It must be someone's job

to pop the heads on Christ bobbles
on the line, to pour light into a mold

and smoke an American Spirit
on lunch and believe

in a union. Every faith is looking for
something too big to see. The common

names of our common demons are Kinked-
Waterhose and Gnat-Up-the-Nose,

Haven't-Any and Get-Away. I brush
away my angel

of dandruff. My only devil
is a beam of light

through the driver's side
window that falls on my shoulder

for only as long
as the sun remains

in one place or the road stays
straight and narrow.

Cartography in Absentia

The friend you seldom see becomes a stranger
        at once when you remember him while together
you eat lunch in late summer on the sidewalk
        outside a café in the delible shade of an umbrella.
The shadow, slimming, urges you closer together
        in your uncomfortable chairs, as if this clement
course of acquaintance is like a river changing

        its bearing by flooding its banks
and spreading over the flatlands to fill
        the shy valleys so it forgets itself, and looking out
across the surface of its waters, it cannot
        tell what, if any part, was among its first current,
and neither can it remember where it grooved to start,
        and so, drying up, pinches away oxbows of *this one*
time and *once,* and *once again,* and leaves them

        for good. And in the minute which is too long to hold
a camera on you paused at the azalea
        in the cemetery where you walked alone, you couldn't
map it among his motives, couldn't inhabit his momentum
        of thought that seemed to end just beyond the edge of the world.

But if you stop now and hold back
        memory and say *No more for now* before spinning
your life like a globe of wildly colored countries
        and continents that once existed in a single mass,
closing your eyes and holding your finger above
        the blurred sphere until the moment,
by chance, you choose to make land on a past
        instant, ask yourself: *What memories did I have then?*
Can you know?

You can say *this happened* and *this happened*
and *this, this*. But it doesn't add up to the whole
          just as the shadow and the light doesn't
make the sun; or, it erodes if you try to
          trace the long shore of What Was, which is why you avoid
each other's eyes, rebuilding, as you must, your flooded
          towns of knowledge into small talk and small bites
and, finally, a quick *Good-bye!...*

          And anyway, memory is not a globe
though you bathe in its cold waters
          as it spins and turns and turns away and back
again so that no matter which way you leave
          the sunny café, parting or not, you're always
moving toward the edge and over it.

Aubade

Sometimes we say to one
        a goodbye
        meant for another. Morning
and the meperidine dream
            breaks to shaking. My husband

guides me by his hands
        on my
        hips like a window-
dresser wheeling a mannequin
            into sunlight, toward its reflection. I dreamt

of being, like fruit,
        faceless.
        The surgeon insists it's
the swelling. He must've learned
            to stitch on the flesh of an

orange, unless this idea is an ambrosia
        the gods pretend
        to eat so that when we steal,
we steal pathetically.
            The bath reminds me

of a lover. The meperidine
        guides me by its
        hands on
the glass. He holds my head as if a baby's
            and tilts me back. I dreamed of being faceless

like morning. The bath reminds me
of a window. The dream—
it breaks like a stitch....
Sometimes we say to one the goodbye
another meant.

Pastoral (Radio)

Out of range the stations' signals confuse—

    like grasses, crossing. Over the fields,

        a field of waves. I have thrown my voice into

    the future. I've called after

it to return. Like the radio,

    I'm waiting for something to come, flickering

meanwhile with half-songs.

Supine Body in Full-Length Mirror, Hotel Room, Upper West Side

All is seen.
—Dante's Virgil

What startles first is that it's there.

After long hours in the car

when thought seemed
seamless with forward

motion, & the body,

a home you left that morning—

& now it's naked & unyielding,

a narrative,
if you'll have it

that the scars know more
about your past

than you choose to remember—

exact angle & slip
of a blade

in your cheek you've spent
months trying to douse

in the gasoline

of a better story.

& the stretch marks
rivuleting your breasts, the body's

erasive white-
washing, the blot

where your aureola was once
pink. It takes

imagination to say that what's there
in the mirror

is what's you—

which is why most creatures don't
feel guilt.

& if they have

memories, the form wriggling
in that claw-trap

is another
member of the flock,

witnessed. & the doves they released

over your brother's grave wear
symbolism like buckshot

in the breast,

unknowingly.

Such dirty things
        meaning purity.

All those you've called you.

Notes

The book's epigraphs are taken from Dante's *Inferno* (trans. Musa, modified with the aid of Pinsky's translation) and *Wise Blood*, John Huston's 1979 film based on Flannery O'Connor's novel, starring Brad Dourif as Hazel Motes.

pg. 3
"Reading Ovid at the Plastic Surgeon's" takes its epigraph from Elizabeth Bishop's "In the Waiting Room" and its quoted text from David Raeburn's translation of Ovid's *Metamorphoses* (Penguin).

pg. 9
"Wheelchair in a Hayloft" takes its epigraph from "Good Country People" by Flannery O'Connor.

pg. 18
"The Bright Obvious" takes its title from "Man Carrying Thing" by Wallace Stevens.

pg. 38
Cops was a 1989–2013 Fox documentary show that followed police officers.

pg. 41
"Pretty Polly" is a traditional murder ballad. Listen to Dock Boggs's versions.

pg. 42
"All These Things Shall Be Added Unto You" takes its title from Matthew 6:33.

pg. 46
"Tomography" is a category of wave imagining that includes PET scans.

pg. 56
Athena, disguised as a girl, leads Odysseus to the Court of Alcinous of Phaeacia, where he admires the orchards.

pg. 58
Bruce Bickford is best known for his animation sequences in Frank Zappa's concert film *Baby Snakes*.

pg. 62
On September 19, 2007, a twin-engine Beechcraft King Air crashed into Brainerd Village Shopping Center in Chattanooga, Tennessee. All three passengers survived.

pg. 66
Saul Bass was an American graphic designer, illustrator, and animator.

pg. 68
"Roadside America" is an attraction in Shartlesville, Pennsylvania, which boasts "The World's Greatest Indoor Miniature Village." The epigraph is from Martory's poem "the why of the meadows" (trans. Ashbery).

pg. 76
"Supine Body in Full-Length Mirror, Hotel Room, Upper West Side" was conceived as a response to a trip I took alone a month after my brother's death and the following year's diagnosis of cancer. I had been rereading Dante, and looking at a body—even one's own body—in the hotel room's mirror seemed a lot like having to climb Lucifer: enormous, world-skewing. Hell to purgatory, the self emerging.

Acknowledgments

These poems originally appeared in the following publications, sometimes in different forms and with different titles.

Agni: "Stopping at Texaco a Year After My Brother's Death" and "The Wind Lends a Voice to the Mountain Laurel Above Pretty Polly's Grave"

Barn Owl Review: "Abstinence Lesson"

Blackbird: "Pastoral (Future Interstate)," "Pastoral (Radio)," and "Pastoral (With One's Head out the Car Window)"

The Collagist: "Paradiso"

Colorado Review: "YouTube: Dog Eating a Human Leg on the Ganges"

cream city review: "Tomography"

The Freeman: "Aubade"

Green Mountains Review Online: "Groundspeed"

Harvard Review: "The Showers"

Linebreak: "Entente"

iO: "The Bright Obvious" and "Cartography in Absentia"

Miramar: "Bruce Bickford at the Edge of the World" and "Life Vest Under Your Seat"

Narrative: "Snake Woman"

New England Review: "Supine Body in Full-Length Mirror, Hotel Room, Upper West Side"

The Paris-American: "Strata"

Ploughshares: "Static, Frequency"

Poetry: "Reading Ovid at the Plastic Surgeon's" and "Saul Bass Redesigns the First Man"

Poetry Northwest: "Wheelchair in a Hayloft"

Southern Indiana Review: "The Rising Cost of Dying"

Third Coast: "Pastoral (Oncoming)"

Vinyl: "The Episode of *Cops* in Which My Father Appears" and "Roadside America"

Waxwing: "All These Things Shall Be Added Unto You" and "Phaeacia's Orchard"

"YouTube: Dog Eating a Human Leg on the Ganges" also appeared in the chapbook *Bestiary of Gall* (Sundress Publications, 2013).

Loving thanks to Jeremy and my family; my MFA teachers David Wojahn, Kathy Graber, and Greg Donovan; mentors Claudia Emerson, Tom Sleigh, Linda Bierds, and Mary Szybist; my friend-family Gregory Kimbrell, Joey Kingsley, Lena Moses-Schmitt, and Tracy Tanner; friends and champions Angela Apte, Amy Arthur, Amanda Bausch, Jocelyn Casey-Whiteman, George David and Elisabeth Clark, Denise Dicks, Caitlin Doyle, Keith Ekiss, Tarfia Faizullah, Mary Flinn, Jonathan Heinen, Jenny Johnson, Michael Keller, Katelyn Kiley, Ross Losapio, Lea Marshall, Randy Marshall, Sebastian Matthews, Nick McRae, Tomás Morín, Annie Rudy, R. Dale Smith, Bri Spicer, Ryan Teitman and Julia Eckhardt, Patrick Scott Vickers, Susan Settlemyre Williams; my editor Mary Biddinger, designer Amy Freels, and artist Hollie Chastain; and the organizations that have sustained me directly and indirectly in writing this book, including 32 *Poems*, Virginia Commonwealth University, Tinker Mountain Writers' Workshop, Bread Loaf Writers' Conference, Sewanee Writers' Conference, Kenyon Review Writers' Workshop, Gettysburg College, William & Mary, Centenary College, and the University of Akron Press.

Photo: Tracy Tanner

Emilia Phillips is the author of the two poetry collections, *Signaletics* (2013) and *Groundspeed* (2016) from the University of Akron Press, and three chapbooks including *Beneath the Ice Fish Like Souls Look Alike* (Bull City Press, 2015). Her poetry appears in *Agni, Gulf Coast, Harvard Review, The Kenyon Review, New England Review, Ploughshares, Poetry,* and elsewhere. She has received fellowships to Bread Loaf Writers' Conference, The Kenyon Review Writers Workshop, U.S. Poets in Mexico, and Vermont Studio Center; the 2013–2014 Emerging Writer Lectureship at Gettysburg College; and the 2012 Poetry Prize from *The Journal.* She has taught at The College of William & Mary, Gettysburg College, Tinker Mountain Writers' Workshop, and Virginia Commonwealth University. She's the Assistant Professor of Creative Writing at Centenary College in Hackettstown, NJ.